GREAT BATTLES

Jane A. C. West

Rising Stars UK Ltd.
22 Grafton Street, London W1S 4EX
www.risingstars-uk.com

nasen
Helping Everyone Achieve

NASEN House, 4/5 Amber Business Village, Amber Close, Amington, Tamworth, Staffordshire B77 4RP

Published 2008

Series Consultant: Lorraine Petersen
Cover design: Neil Straker Creative
Cover photograph: Alamy
Design: Clive Sutherland
Editorial: Frances Ridley
Illustrations: Bill Greenhead for Illustration Ltd
Photographs: AKG Images: 4, 6, 7, 14, 20, 30, 35, 46
Alamy: 6, 7, 11, 16, 178, 26-27, 36, 45
The Art Archive: 6, 8, 23, 33, 38, 39, 40-41, 43, 44-45, 47
Getty Images: 24
Kobal Collection: 7, 28-29

British Library Cataloguing in Publication Data.
A CIP record for this book is available from the British Library.

ISBN: 978-1-84680-447-2

Printed by: Craftprint International Ltd, Singapore

Jane West would like to thank Roger Crawley for his advice on 'the greatest weapon'.

Contents

GREAT BATTLES: THE BIG PICTURE

Battles are bloody and people die but battles can still be 'great'. They are 'great' because of the things we remember them for: great bravery, great daring or, sometimes, great loss.

Find the answers to these questions.

1. Who tried and failed to force the Romans out of Britain?
2. Which new weapon helped the Turkish army beat the Greeks?
3. How old was the Red Baron when he died?

Air Aces
Fast, deadly and dangerous combat.

The Battle of Little Bighorn
Victory for the Indians.

The Battle of Trafalgar
Nelson beats the French.

Ambush!
Surprise attacks don't always succeed.

The Battle of Watling Street
Boudica's last stand.

The Battle of Stirling Bridge
A Scottish hero is born.

The Siege of Constantinople
A new weapon shows its power.

Boadicea, Queen of the Iceni.

Published June 1 1815, by R. Havell. 3, Chapel Street, London.

THE WARRIOR QUEEN

Boudica lived in Britain nearly 2000 years ago. At this time, the **Romans** ruled Britain. Boudica was a Queen of the **Iceni** tribe. Her name meant 'victory' in Celtic. She hated the Romans for treating her people like slaves. She wanted to fight back.

WANTED!

BOUDICA – QUEEN OF THE ICENI TRIBE

CRIMES:

REBELLION AGAINST ROMAN RULE.
BURNING COLCHESTER TO THE GROUND.
SETTING FIRE TO LONDON AND ST ALBANS.
MURDERING ROMAN PEOPLE.

BOUDICA HAS DESTROYED THREE GREAT, PEACEFUL **ROMAN** CITIES. SHE HAS LED HER TRIBE INTO BATTLE AGAINST US. EVEN NOW HER SOLDIERS ARE GETTING READY TO FIGHT AGAIN. WE ROMANS MUST AND WILL BEAT HER.

LOYAL ROMANS – WE NEED YOUR HELP. ROMAN RULE AND ROMAN LAW MUST BE OBEYED.

HAVE YOU SEEN THIS WOMAN?

1.8 METRES TALL

LONG, RED, CURLY HAIR

FIERCE EYES HARSH VOICE

WEARS GOLD TORC NECKLACE

DRESSES IN LONG, COLOURFUL ROBES

Reward: 500 denarii* for capture of this British beast.

* A Roman soldier was paid 300 **denarii** a year.

The Battle of Watling Street, 61 AD

The Romans had to stop Boudica before other tribes joined the rebellion. The Romans and the Iceni met at the Battle of Watling Street. Before the battle Boudica said:

"Win the battle or die. That is what I, a woman, will do."

Boudica's army was destroyed in the battle. Afterwards, Boudica killed herself by taking poison.

The Romans ruled England and Wales for the next 350 years. Nobody dared fight the Roman army again.
A statue of Boudica stands in Westminster, London.

A SCOTTISH HERO

The film *Braveheart* is about the Battle of Stirling Bridge. It doesn't get all the facts right, but the film has a great hero – just like the real battle. His name was William Wallace.

The National Wallace Monument

The Wallace Monument is a great place to visit. It was built in 1874 and is six metres high. It is built on top of Abbey Craig hill near Stirling.

Enjoy the view from the top of the Monument.

Learn about the Battle of Stirling Bridge and its hero, William Wallace.

In 1297 the English, King Edward I, ruled Scotland.

The Scottish wanted to be free so William Wallace started a rebellion. The English sent their army to fight the Scots. They thought they would win.

60,000 English soldiers faced 40,000 Scots led by William Wallace at the Battle of Stirling Bridge.

The Scots attacked from the top of Abbey Craig.

The Battle of Stirling Bridge, 11th September 1297

KEY

1	The English army reached the River Forth. They had to cross the river to go any further.
2	There was only one narrow bridge. The English army began to cross it.
3	Wallace and the Scottish army waited at the top of a hill.
4	The Scottish army let half the English army cross the river.
5	Then the Scottish army rushed down the hill and burned the bridge.
6	The English were trapped. It was a great victory for the Scots.

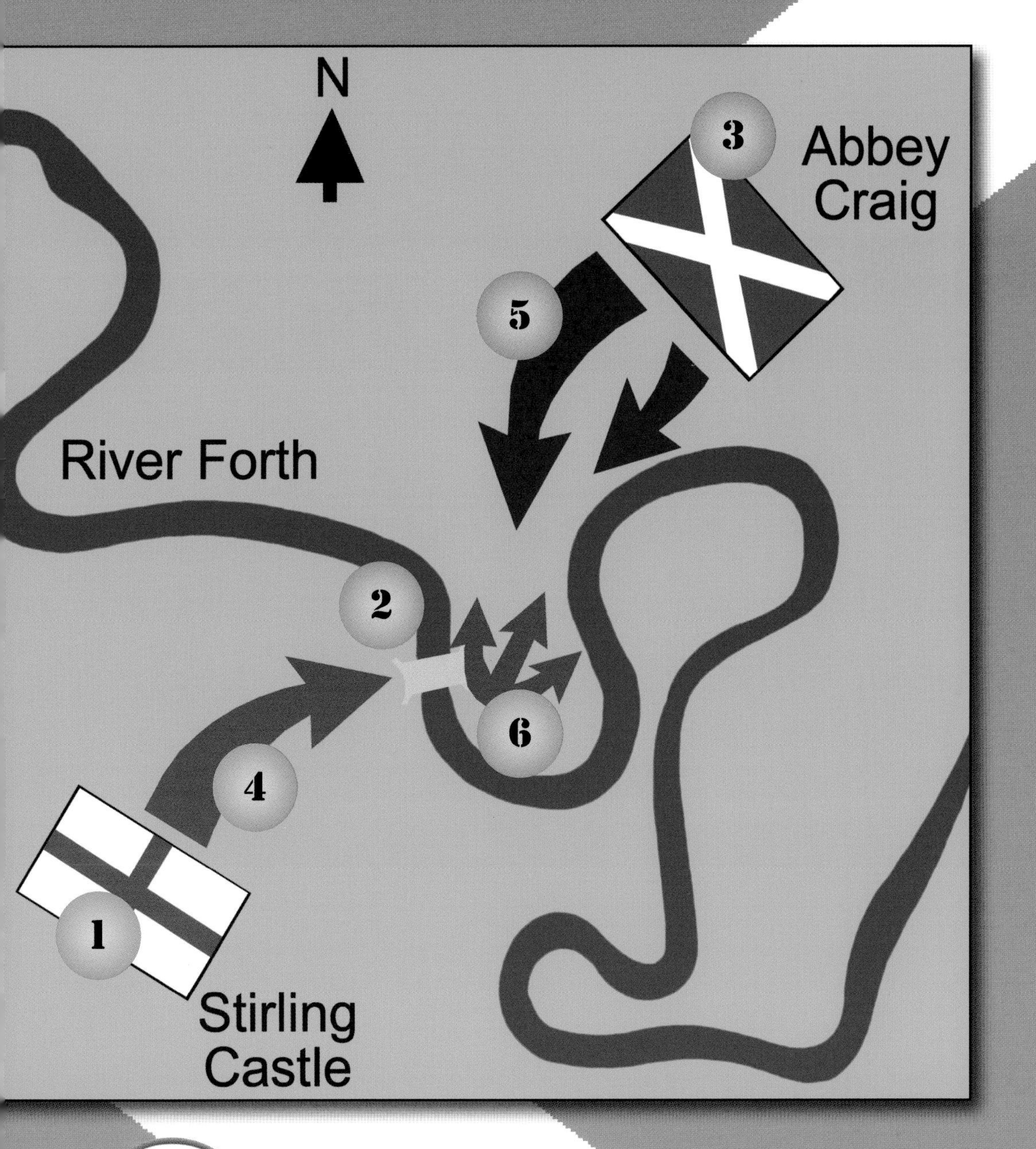

One year later the English defeated the Scots at the Battle of Falkirk. William Wallace was **executed**.

THE GREATEST WEAPON

In 1453, the king of Turkey and his army laid **siege** to the city of Constantinople. For 54 days, 7,000 Greek soldiers held off 100,000 Turkish troops. The Turks won because they had a powerful new weapon – a huge **cannon**.

SUPERGUN SMASHES CITY WALLS!

*Turks use biggest **siege cannon** the world has ever seen!*

The Turks are battering the city walls of Constantinople into rubble. They are using a huge siege cannon.

It's nine metres long and is big enough for a man to crawl inside! This amazing weapon can fire a 680 kg cannonball one mile.

BUT IT'S NOT ALL GOOD NEWS FOR THE TURKS!

- The cannon is very heavy – over 25 tonnes. It takes 400 men and 60 **oxen** to move it.
- The Turks have to build a road to Constantinople to move the cannon.
- The cannon takes three hours to reload. It's also very difficult to aim.
- The Turks are running out of cannonballs – they may have to use rocks!

The Battle for Constantinople, 29th May 1453

Constantinople was a rich and important **trading centre**. It was a **fortress** city protected by thick stone walls. The Turks' great cannon broke through the stone walls. Each day more of the old city walls crumbled.

The siege lasted for 54 days. Then the Turkish troops attacked by land and sea. They defeated the Greeks and drove them from the city. The Turks gave Constantinople a new name – Istanbul.

The city is still called Istanbul. You can still see the ruins of the walls today.

CLOSE-UP: AMBUSH!

Hannibal **ambushed** the Romans over 2000 years ago. He and his army crossed the mountains called the Alps in winter – and they took 37 elephants with them! Hannibal's army won a great victory because they took the Romans by surprise.

The Zulu tribe led a surprise attack on the English in 1879. The battle took place at Rorke's Drift in South Africa. Only 139 British soldiers fought 5,000 Zulus. The British side held out until more soldiers arrived to save them.

BATTLE AT SEA

In 1805, Napoleon wanted to invade Britain. He moved his soldiers onto ships at Cape Trafalgar near Spain. The ships were going to take the soldiers to invade Britain.

Napoleon's **fleet** had to be stopped. So the British Navy, led by Lord Nelson, came up with a daring plan.

Daily Battle Report

7th November 1805

Sixteen days ago, British ships beat French and Spanish warships in a battle at Cape Trafalgar. Lord Nelson's daring battle plan has saved us from Napoleon. But we have paid a high price for our victory.

Lord Nelson sent this message to his fleet before the battle:

"England expects every man to do his duty."

Lord Nelson led his fleet bravely. At 1.15p.m. his left shoulder was hit by a French **musket ball**. It passed through his lung and broke his back.

Three hours later, Lord Nelson was dead.

His last words were: "Thank God I have done my duty".

> "My ears rang with the shrieks of the wounded and the moans of the dying."
>
> Royal Marine Paul Harris Nicholls, age 16
>
> *Eyewitness account*

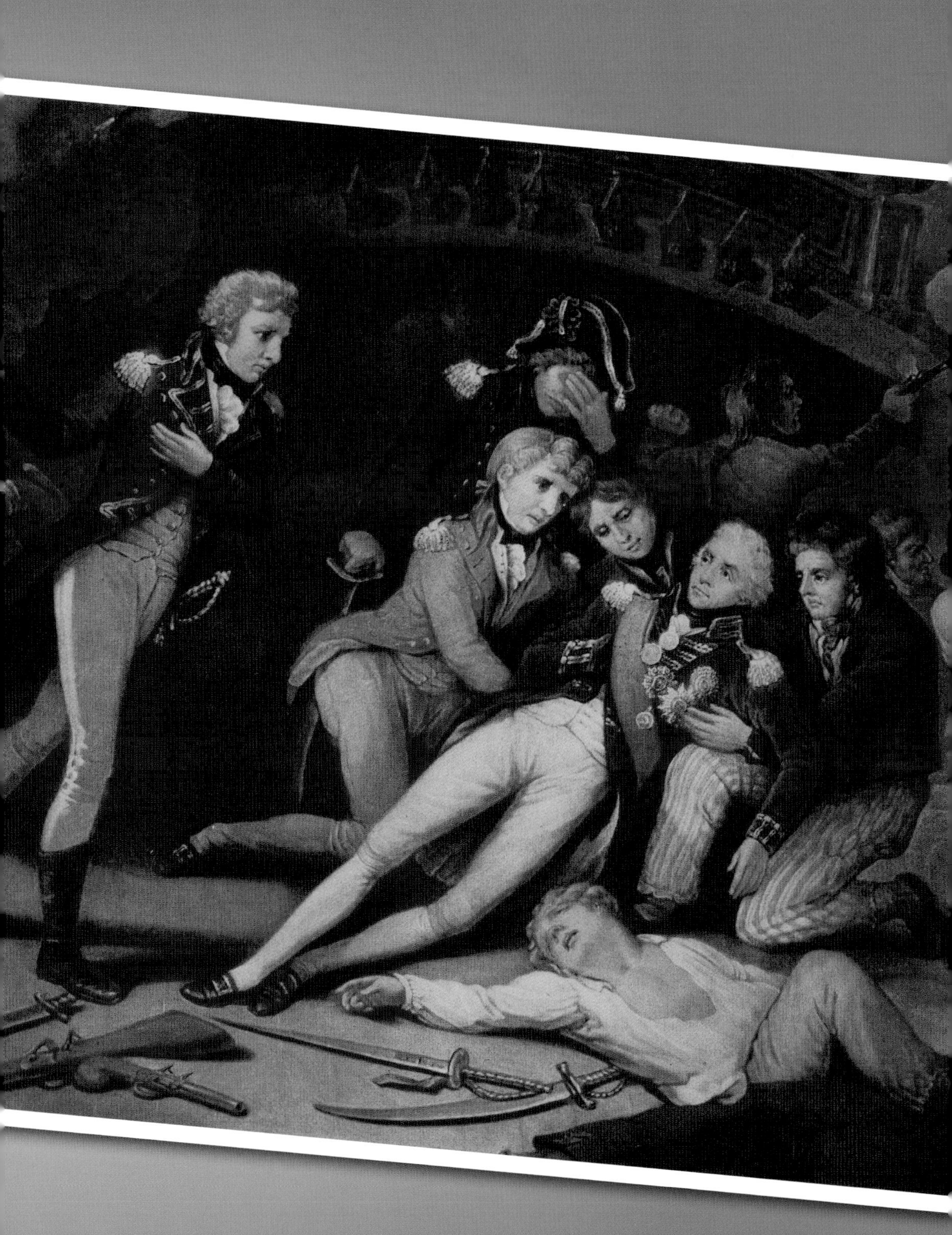

The Battle of Trafalgar, 21st October 1805

The British Navy was led by Lord Nelson. His plan for the Battle of Trafalgar looked like this:

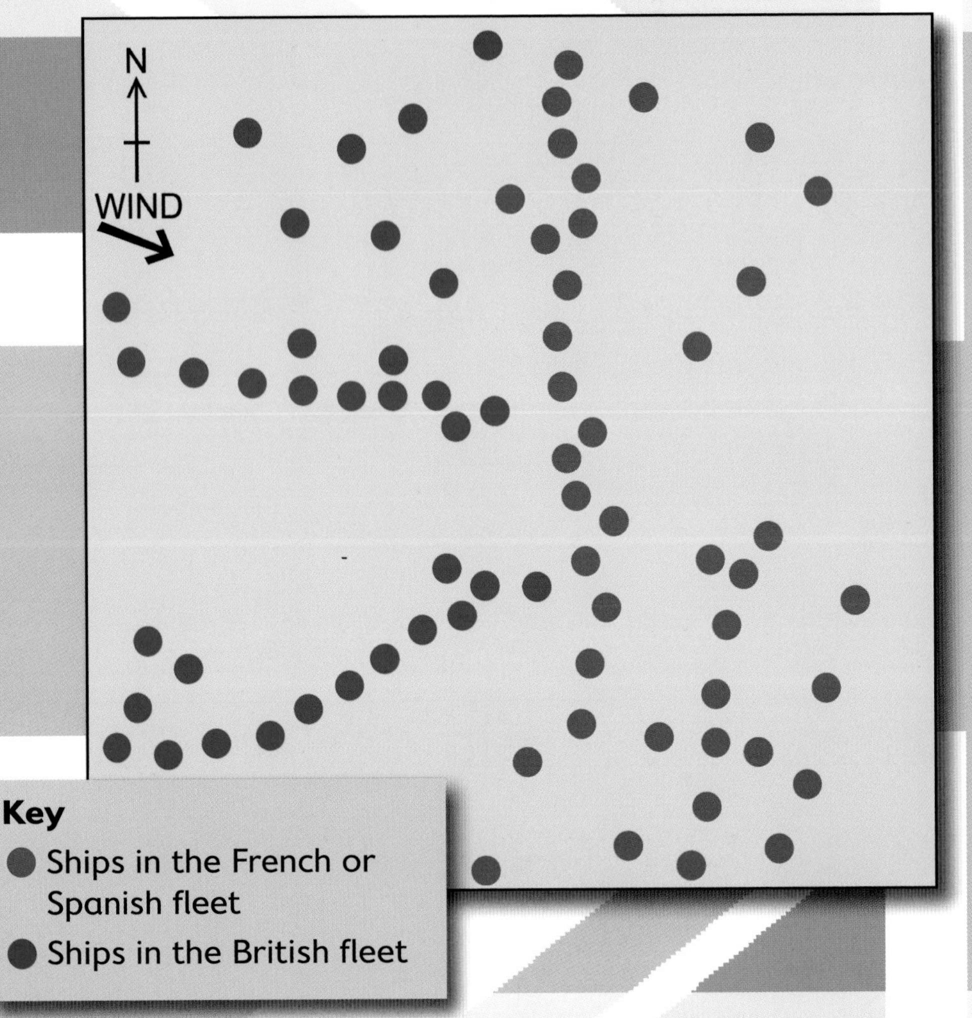

Nelson sailed his ships in two lines towards the enemy **fleet**. The British fleet cut the French fleet in half.

This stopped the French ships sending messages to each other.

The British won a great victory. The French and Spanish lost 22 ships. The British lost no ships – but they did lose a great leader. Lord Nelson died in the battle. It took 16 days for the news to reach Britain.

BATTLE FOR THE WILD WEST

American Indians had lived in the Wild West of America for hundreds of years. But American farmers wanted the Indians' land. The US **Cavalry** was sent to fight the Indians. The two armies met at the Battle of the Little Bighorn.

Battlefield Monthly, Issue 9

The Leaders Talk

Interview: Lieutenant Colonel Custer, 7th Cavalry

Q: Why are you fighting?

A: We want the Indians' land.

Q: You only have 210 men. Is this enough to defeat the Indians?

A: Of course! I am a great leader – it'll be easy.

Colonel Custer

Sioux leader, unconfirmed as Crazy Horse

Interview: Crazy Horse, Chief of the Oglala Sioux

Q: Why are you fighting?

A: To survive. This is our way of life. We don't want to move away from our land.

Q: Can the US cavalry can defeat you?

A: No. We are many – they are few.

Q: What will you do if another army comes after Colonel Custer?

A: We will fight again. We have no choice. If we lose, our way of life will be finished.

BATTLE FACT

The only US survivor was a horse.

The Battle of the Little Bighorn, 26th June 1876

Colonel Custer was an **arrogant** leader. He didn't think it would be hard for the US Army to beat the Indians. He was wrong.

Custer had 210 soldiers and there were nearly 1800 Indians. Custer and his men were outnumbered and outgunned. Every US soldier was killed.

The Indians won this battle but it was their last victory. The US soldiers kept coming. Many Indians were killed. The rest had to live in large camps called **reservations**. They were not allowed to leave.

BATTLE IN THE SKY

In the **First World War**, planes were used in battles for the first time.

The planes were small and fought against each other one on one.

Some pilots became famous for their air battles. They were called **Air Aces**.

The Red Baron

The Red Baron was the most famous Air Ace of the First World War.

He was born in Kleinburg, Germany in 1892. His real name was Manfred von Richthofen. His rich family sent him to military school when he was 11. When the war started he joined a cavalry unit and rode horses.

In 1915, Manfred learned to fly an aeroplane. He joined the Imperial German Army Air Service.

German plane

He fought in hundreds of **dogfights** and shot down about 80 British and French planes. People called him The Red Baron because he flew a red plane.

The Red Baron survived for three years as an Air Ace. In April 1918 his plane was shot down and he was killed. He was 25 years old.

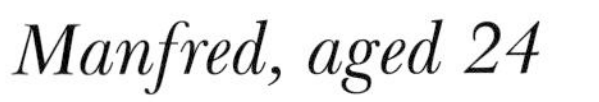

Manfred, aged 24

Air Aces

Life was fast, dangerous and short for pilots in the First World War. Most pilots only survived for a few months.

The planes were made from wood. The **cockpits** were open to rain, wind and bullets.

Pilots threw bricks, chains or rope at their enemy's **propellers**.

At first, pilots carried guns to shoot the enemy's plane. Later, machine guns were fitted into the planes.

Air battles were fast.
It was easy to make a
mistake. And deadly.

GLOSSARY

Air Aces top pilots
Ambush a surprise attack
Arrogant someone who thinks they are better than everybody else
Cavalry soldiers on horses
Cannon a large, heavy gun that fires cannonballs
Cockpit place where the pilot sits in an aeroplane
Denarii Roman coins
Dogfight when two enemy planes fight each other
Executed sentenced to death and killed
First World War a war between many countries, 1914-1918
Fleet a group of ships
Fortress fort or castle
Iceni a tribe that lived in the East of Britain in Roman times
Musket ball a bullet fired from a musket (a type of rifle)
Oxen bulls that carry heavy loads
Propeller the spinning blades on an aeroplane
Rebellion a fight against the government or rulers of the country
Reservation an area of land where Indians were told they had to live
Romans people from the city of Rome in Italy. 2,000 years ago they had a huge empire.
Siege when an enemy army surrounds a fort and cuts off food and supplies
Torc a necklace in the shape of a letter 'C'
Trading centre where business takes place

INDEX